S0-AAG-399

# Magic Tricks

igloo

This edition published in 2011
by Igloo Books Ltd
Cottage Farm
Sywell
NN6 0BJ

www.igloo-books.com

Copyright © 2007 Igloo Books Ltd

All rights reserved. No part of this publication may be reproduced,
stored in a retrieval system, or transmitted in any way or by
any means, electronic, mechanical, photocopying, recording or
otherwise, without the prior written permission of the publisher.

Cataloguing in Publication Data information

B044 0611

10 9 8 7 6 5

ISBN: 978-1-84561-711-0

Printed and manufactured in China

Produced by Metro Media Ltd
Author: Marc Dominic

Photography by Christopher & Anna Bond/Paula Smith
With thanks to: Jo St Mart, Cyrups Hayley, Celia Hart
Other images: clipart.com

### DISCLAIMER
The author, publisher and their agent have made every effort to
ensure the content of this book was accurate at the time of publication.
The author, publisher and their agent cannot be held liable for any
errors and omissions in the publication or actions that may be taken
as a consequence of using it.
Ensure that all objects used for the tricks are kept away from young
children and babies. Any tricks using balloons should be supervised by
an adult, as children under the age of 8 can choke or suffocate
on uninflated or broken balloons. Ensure that any thread and
rubber bands are disposed of after use.

Magic has always fascinated people, from the Ancient Egyptians, and the Greeks and Romans, to modern TV audiences. Each generation has had a great, world-famous magician, from Dante and Houdini, through Harry Blackstone to David Copperfield and David Blaine. But magic is an art full of secrets, and learning it can seem difficult. Magic books can be wordy and full of tricks that aren't fun to do – we hope you'll find this book is different.

Each chapter reveals a group of tricks with something in common. Each trick is graded by its WOW! factor (how impressive the trick is), how much time it takes to learn, and how technical and difficult it is. So you can pick the easy ones first if you wish.

However, when learning, remember the golden rule – practice, practice, practice and, when you think you're ready, practice some more!

Then, when you really are ready, show your magic and enjoy it but don't give away the secrets – even to friends. Once someone knows the method, the trick loses its appeal.

When you learn tricks, try and think up different ways of presenting them. Imitating a TV magician is great but you will always be a copy, and we want you to become a great magician in your own right. But, most of all, have fun and enjoy performing and practicing. Welcome to the wonderful world of magic!

# CHAPTER 1

This chapter is full of impromptu stunts and effects that you can do using mainly your hands and fingers.

Some look like feats of an extreme physical nature, others are silly little effects you can do anywhere – when you're in the school yard or at a soccer game, for instance.

These tricks teach some of the basics of magic, about audience control and the use of language. Many are visual and need practice and 'selling' to the audience.

If, when you try them, they don't work, think about the reasons. Did you rush it? Did you tell the audience what was going to happen before you achieved the effect?

There are lots of tricks of the trade you can develop from this chapter, so have a look, it's easy – the harder stuff comes later!

Remember that, no matter how simple the trick, it needs practice, practice and more practice. When you think you have it, get someone to watch and ask them what was wrong with the effect. There will be some good points but you need to know the bad points to make it better. Write the comments down and then try and make improvements – and then practice some more.

Remember, magic is about performance.

# DETACHABLE THUMB

## Effect

You appear to remove the end of your thumb, moving it back and forth along your hand or lifting it up.

| | | |
|---|---|---|
| Wow factor | ★ ★ ★ ★ ★ | |
| Performance skills | ★ ★ ★ ★ ★ | |
| Skill | ★ ★ ★ ★ ★ | |
| Time to learn | 15 mins | |
| Set up time | None needed | |

Simply hold out one hand sideways with the palm out and the tip of the thumb folded down behind the hand.

**1**

**2**

Then bend your other thumb, and place it so that the tip appears to be connected to the folded-down thumb, with the forefinger bent to cover the joint.

**3**

Slowly slide your two hands across each other and the thumb appears to slide off.

### TOP TIP!
This is a simple effect to do but you must get the angle of vision right for the spectator. Don't show it for too long as you'll be discovered!

---

# ELEVEN FINGERS EFFECT

The art of magic often involves the seeming ability to defy the laws of logic. With this stunt you can convince your friends that you have eleven fingers!

| | | |
|---|---|---|
| Wow factor | ★ ★ ★ ★ ★ | |
| Performance skills | ★ ★ ★ ★ ★ | |
| Skill | ★ ★ ★ ★ ★ | |
| Time to learn | 15 mins | |
| Set up time | None needed | |

Using your right forefinger to point with, touch each finger of your left hand, counting out loud, "One, two, three, four, five."

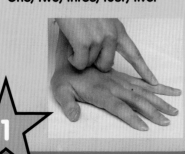

**1**

Then with your left forefinger count the fingers on your right hand, "Six, seven, eight, nine, ten."

**2**

Say, "Funny, I know I had eleven. Let's try again". This time count backwards, pointing to the fingers of the left hand, and say, "Ten, nine, eight, seven, six....". Hold up your left hand and say, "Six fingers on this hand and..". Then hold up your right hand and say, "Five fingers on this hand. So five plus six makes eleven!"

**3**

# DO AS I DO

## Effect

This is a great effect and makes the magician appear double-jointed. Follow the arm with gray sleeves.

★ **1**

You ask the spectator to copy you and extend your right arm – thumb pointing up to the ceiling with the fingers spread.

★ **2**

Rotate your wrist counterclockwise so your thumb now points to the floor.

★ **3**

Extend your left hand and spread your fingers.

★ **4**

Pass the left hand over the top of your right hand and turn it clockwise so the thumbs are together.

Grasp your hands together and hold the fingers tight – now you do the secret bit.

★ **5**

# DO AS I DO - SECRET BIT

| Wow factor | ★ ★ ★ ★ ★ |
|---|---|
| Performance skills | ★ ★ ★ ★ ★ |
| Skill | ★ ★ ★ ★ ★ |
| Time to learn | 30 mins |
| Set up time | None needed |

**6**

As the spectator grabs their hands together, let go with your left hand and reach out and ask the spectator to hold their hands tight. If several people are doing this, squeeze a few of their hands gently.

**7**

As you replace your left hand, instead of going over your right hand you come underneath and rotate your wrist counterclockwise with your thumbs together.

**8**

To make your arms look similar to the spectator's, push your left elbow across your chest to try and touch the right elbow.

**9**

Now ask them to copy you as you roll your wrists and open up your elbows so it looks like your hands are clasped in front of you with untwisted arms.

**TOP TIP!**
Do not repeat this trick too often or make your move and replacement too obvious – it will give the game away.

The spectator will be tied in knots!

**10**

## Effect

This is a strange effect, where you appear to get a large crack when you move your neck or shoulder. You need a small plastic cup.

| | | |
|---|---|---|
| Wow factor | | ★★★ ★ ★ |
| Performance skills | | ★ ★ ★ ★ ★ |
| Skill | | ★ ★ ★ ★ ★ |
| Time to learn | 15 mins | |
| Set up time | 1 min | |

**1**

You need a small plastic cup, which you place under your right arm.

**2**

Place your left hand on your neck or shoulder and pretend to make a funny or awkward move.

**3**

As you do this, squeeze your right bicep into your body to crush the plastic cup. This will make a number of snapping sounds. Shake your shoulder or neck slightly as you say something like, "That's better."

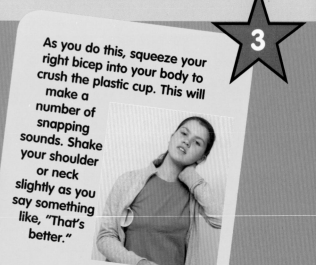

# INVISIBLE STRENGTH

You appear to wind an imaginary thread around your finger. As you do, the spectator feels their fingers pulled together.

| | | |
|---|---|---|
| Wow factor | | ★★ ★ ★ ★ |
| Performance skills | | ★ ★ ★ ★ ★ |
| Skill | | ★ ★ ★ ★ ★ |
| Time to learn | 15 mins | |
| Set up time | None needed | |

**1**

Ask your friend to fold their hands together, weaving the fingers and clasping them tightly.

**2**

After a few moments of doing this, tell them to raise their two index (first) fingers so that they are sticking up, about an inch apart (a 'church and steeple' effect).

**3**

Now, slowly move your hands up over their hands (but don't touch them). As you circle their fingers with your hand, slowly, but inevitably, your friend's fingers will start to move together. Tell them to concentrate on their fingers and soon their fingers will touch.

## THUMB GRAB

This is a different thumb trick. Hold your left hand with the thumb pointing up. Grab your left thumb with your right fist. As you do this, push your left thumb right down into the palm of your hand. Do this as soon as the right hand grabs the left thumb and covers it from view. Then move your right fist and appear to pull your thumb off!

## HOLE IN THE HAND

For this you need a tube, for example a toilet roll. Hold the tube up to your right eye and close your left eye. Now open your left eye and hold your left hand upright with the palm facing you. Place it next to the end of the tube and an optical illusion is created. It looks like you can see a hole in your palm.

## STRONG ARM

This is an old yoga and martial arts trick. Have someone hold out their arm parallel with the floor. See what happens when you try and push it down – it moves. Now ask them to do the same but to close their eyes, imagine they are a strong statue and that there is a surge of energy, like steel rods coming up from the floor, through their body and out along the arm. As the rods come through their arm they twist and actually become strong. Then try to push their arm down like before – it will be very strong and much harder to move. Weird!

## TWO LITTLE DICKIE BIRDS

This uses the children's nursery rhyme Two Little Dickie Birds and is a cute trick – ideal for younger brothers and sisters.

'Two little dickie birds sitting on a wall,
One named Peter, one named Paul.
Fly away Peter, fly away Paul,
Come back Peter, come back Paul!'

On each index finger put a small sticker or a piece of paper with a face on it. As you say the rhyme, raise a left hand for Peter and a right hand for Paul. When you say 'Fly away Peter', the left hand is thrown in the air and brought back down. As you do this, quickly bend the index finger into the palm to hide it, and extend the middle finger so it looks like the paper or sticker has vanished. For 'Fly away Paul' do the same with the right hand. To make them come back, reverse the action.

## THE JUMPING FINGER

Here you create an illusion that a finger jumps from one hand to the other. Extend the first fingers of both hands, with the other fingers tucked underneath, and wave the hands slightly from side to side. Then move the right hand to the left so the hands touch and, as they touch, curl the first finger of the right hand underneath and extend the second finger of the left hand so it looks like the finger has jumped across. Reverse the action to make it jump back again.

# CHAPTER 2

Money provides a great tool for magic tricks, with its variety of coin sizes and notes. It is also important to everybody
– we all use it every day.

Every nation has a currency but, be aware, some don't have coins now. If you use coins that are not from the spectators' country – for example using a 50 cent piece in London – remember to explain why: "Dad got me these when he was in New York and they are magic."

All the tricks and moves in this chapter will need practice, and some need preparation. But, be careful. If you can do a coin roll with a 50 cent piece or a £2 coin, it doesn't mean that you could do it with a quarter or 10p piece. The coins are different and feel different when you use them, so try and make sure you practice with the coin you want to use.

Making a coin vanish and then pulling it from your ear is often the first trick a child sees, probably performed by a family member.
If you come away with one good trick from this book, I would recommend a coin trick.

But be careful – if you ask to borrow money to do your trick always ensure you give it back! If you get the coin wet or messy, offer to give them a clean one if they prefer.

Practice well and in no time you'll be making coins bend and even making them vanish!

## Effect

This is a simple but very effective trick. You borrow a coin and then, rubbing it gently, appear to make it bend as if made of rubber. Dimes and quarters in the US or 10p and 50p coins in the UK, work best.

| | | |
|---|---|---|
| Wow factor | | ★★ ★ ★ ★ |
| Performance skills | | ★★ ★ ★ ★ |
| Skill | | ★ ★ ★ ★ ★ |
| Time to learn | 15 mins | |
| Set up time | None needed | |

**1**

Hold the coin with both hands, with your thumbs on the back of the coin, and the first and second fingers on the front. Try and get as much of the coin's surface as you can. The best way to do this is to push the thumbs forward and pull the fingers to the edge of the coin.

Move both your hands inwards so that the backs of your hands move forward and towards each other. Your thumbs should stay on the coin at all times. Then, move the hands back into the start position.

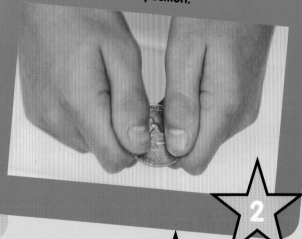

**2**

**3**

Repeat this four or five times in a rhythmic motion. The coin will appear to bend. As you get used to it, you will find that your grip will loosen and you will become more relaxed.

## TOP TIP!

You need to not overplay this effect as it relies on an optical illusion. Make it look like hard work at first and, as it appears to get easier, you can speed up the moves.

## Effect

As much as this is a magic trick it more of a stunt using money. You take a piece of paper money: a dollar bill or a £5 note, and then prove you can balance a coin or on its edge.

| Wow factor | ★★★★★ |
|---|---|
| Performance skills | ★★★★★ |
| Skill | ★★★★★ |
| Time to learn | 15 mins |
| Set up time | None needed |

**2**

Take the note and lay it flat on a table. Then start at the short edge and fold it over ½in/1cm towards you. Crease it hard.

**1**

Turn the note over and do the same.

**3**

Repeat action 1 & 2 until the whole note is folded, like a concertina.

**4**

Slowly allow the note to unfold.

Stand the note on one of its long edges. Slowly balance a large coin on the top edge.

**5**

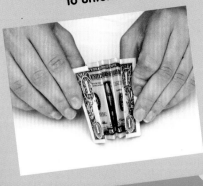

### TOP TIP!
This can be done as a bet, if you like. For it to work, it is best to use a crisp note or a newish note, not an old one. Make sure you practice with the object you expect to balance. Different notes from different countries support different weights.

Extra Trick!
Instead of a coin, use a small glass.

## Effect

You explain you have wonderful skills of dexterity. You can balance a coin on your fingertips, or on another coin, and no one else will be able to copy this amazing feat!

| Wow factor | ★ ★ ★ ★ ★ |
|---|---|
| Performance skills | ★ ★ ★ ★ ★ |
| Skill | ★ ★ ★ ★ ★ |
| Time to learn | 30 mins |
| Set up time | None needed |

**1** Using a regular straight pin or cocktail stick, stand it between two fingers (as shown). This is the upright position. Push it back so it lies between your fingers.

**2** Take out the coin. Lay the coin down on top of the cocktail stick in your other hand.

**3** Raise the coin to a standing position near the ends of your fingers and, as you do so, raise the straight cocktail stick with it, making sure no one but you knows the stick is there.

**4** Keep pressure on the cocktail stick between your two fingers, and coin will balance there as if held by unseen forces!

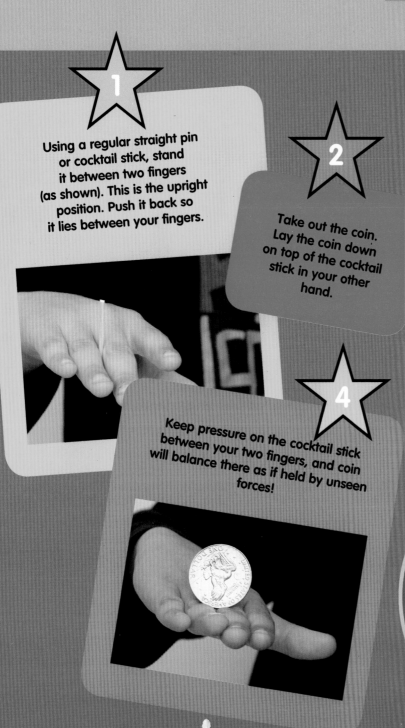

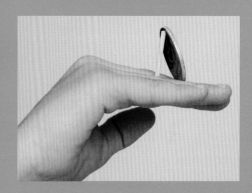

**TOP TIP!**
While you perform this trick, talk about mind over matter or wiggle the fingers of your other hand over the coin as if that was where your power came from! Also, don't forget to dispose of the cocktail stick while people are examining the coin again.

## Effect

A spectator reaches into their pocket and grabs a handful of coins and puts them on the table. You turn your back and they pick up one coin, noting the date on the coin before mixing it up with the rest of the change. You pick up each coin and, by looking at the date, are able to figure out which coin they selected.

| Wow factor | ★★★★★ |
|---|---|
| Performance skills | ★★★★★ |
| Skill | ★★★★★ |
| Time to learn | 45 mins |
| Set up time | None needed |

**1** Ask a spectator to put a handful of coins from their pocket on a table.

**2** Turn your back and ask them to pick one coin up, noting the date on the coin, and then to mix it up with the rest of the change.

Pick up each coin, looking at the dates. Say something like, "This nickel (or 10p piece) was made in 2002. That's interesting, because in 2002 such and such was going on and I just knew that you'd pick it!"

**3**

**4** When you pick up the coins in order to "look at the date", feel the heat of the coins. When someone holds a coin for even just 20 or 30 seconds, the heat from their fingers is transferred to the coin. Not knowing this your audience will be amazed.

### TOP TIP!
If someone guesses that you're feeling which coin is the hottest, you may be able to throw them off the scent by saying, "I wish it were that easy". That indirectly makes them think that they are wrong, and you still have a secret that you are keeping!

## Effect

A fancy coin roll is easier than you think but it takes practice. It is a great way to demonstrate skill at handling coins – and also works well with poker chips!

| | | |
|---|---|---|
| Wow factor | | ★★★★★ |
| Performance skills | | ★★★★★ |
| Skill | | ★★★★★ |
| Time to learn | 3 hours | |
| Set up time | None needed | |

**1**

With the right hand closed and the back of the hand uppermost, show a large coin, such as a 50 cent piece, or £2 coin, pinched flat between the forefinger and the middle finger, and protruding as much as possible.

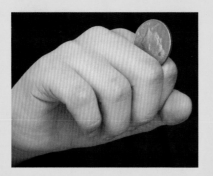

**2**

Push the coin up slightly and release it, permitting the coin to lie down and balance on the back of the middle finger between the knuckles.

Raise the middle finger and bring it down on the right edge of the coin causing it to assume a temporary position pinched flat between the middle and ring (third) fingers.

Without hesitating, the coin is allowed to fall on to the back of the ring finger. The same action is continued until the coin is pinched in a vertical position between the last two fingers.

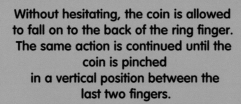

**3**

### Extra Trick!

At this stage of the flourish you may reverse the process, bringing the coin back to its starting position. The normal way to get back to the starting position is to allow the coin to slip between the last two fingers onto the tip of the thumb, which is brought underneath the hand to receive it. It is then carried balanced flat on the ball of the thumb back to its starting place, and the same set of moves repeated as many times as you wish.

### TOP TIP!

After you have learned the basic moves, practice it for hours. Muscle memory is important for this flourish: you must train in your hand to automatically perform all of the moves without hesitating or making a mistake. When you can do it, try one coin in each hand or even two coins in one hand!

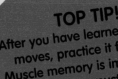

## Effect

The French Drop is one of the oldest techniques used to make a coin vanish. Lots of people can do it badly – practice well and you will be able to perform this trick with any coin, anywhere.

| Wow factor | ★ ★ ★ ★ ★ |
|---|---|
| Performance skills | ★ ★ ★ ★ ★ |
| Skill | ★ ★ ★ ★ ★ |
| Time to learn | 1 hour |
| Set up time | None needed |

**1**

Show a coin by holding it high in the left hand fingertips. Hold the edges and allow a lot of the face of the coin to be seen.

**2**

The right hand approaches the left to supposedly take the coin, the thumb going behind the coin and the fingers in front. As soon as the fingers close around the coin and it is out of sight, allow the coin to fall into the left hand.

**5**

Slowly rub the right-hand fingers as if the coin is dissolving. Then show the coin has vanished.

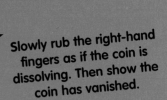

The coin falls between the right thumb and the back of the left fingers. From the front it looks as if you are pinching the coin with your right fingers and thumb.

**3**

Move your right hand up and to the side as the left hand with the coin relaxes. At all times this hand should look natural and not tense.

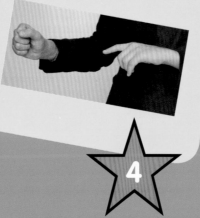

**4**

### TOP TIP!
Practice the natural action of taking the coin and then not taking it, so the moves look identical and fluid.

## Effect

Borrow a coin, and have it marked by a spectator. Then you make it vanish and reappear... inside a bread roll!

| | |
|---|---|
| Wow factor | ★★★★★ |
| Performance skills | ★★★★★ |
| Skill | ★★★★★ |
| Time to learn | 30 minutes |
| Set up time | None needed |

**1**

Ask to borrow a spectator's coin, having them mark it first with a pen. Using the French Drop skill perfected on the opposite page, you will end up with the coin hidden in your right hand.

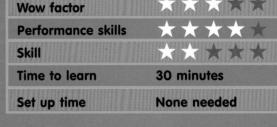

**2**

Take the roll, hold it with two hands so the coin in the fingers of your right hand is under the roll.

Push the coin into the base of the roll. To help do this pull the sides of the roll up. This causes the bottom to split or tear slightly. Push the coin inside, ensuring this is not seen by the audience.

**3**

**4**

To make the coin appear, push the coin with your fingers into the roll, as you now bend the roll in the opposite direction. This tears the roll from the top and closes the gap at the bottom.

The coin now appears to rise to the center of the roll. Ask the spectator to take the coin and check it is the one they marked.

**5**

**TOP TIP!**
Soft rolls are better than hard ones. For a really messy trick, try using a fresh hamburger!

**Extra Trick!**
Try using a real egg and, when the coin is hidden under the egg, crack it into a glass. As you do so, let the coin fall in the glass – it appears to have been in the egg.

# COIN IN ELBOW

## Effect

A coin is displayed and rubbed against the forearm in an attempt to rub it into the arm. After a few failed attempts the coin vanishes. This can be done sitting down or standing behind a table. If you are wearing long sleeves, roll them up.

| | |
|---|---|
| Wow factor | ★★★★★ |
| Performance skills | ★★★★★ |
| Skill | ★★★★★ |
| Time to learn | 1 hour |
| Set up time | None needed |

Take the coin in your left finger. Place your right hand on your shoulder with the forearm facing the audience, elbow pointing down.

**1**

Hold the coin flat between the right forearm and left palm and rub it up and down a few times before letting it slip out, falling to the table. Repeat this action 2 or 3 times.

**2**

Each time you drop the coin, pick it up with the left hand and begin the rubbing process again.

**3**

The last time, pick up the coin with the RIGHT hand. Because they have seen you do it several times before, the audience won't notice that you used the other hand.

**4**

Then, as you lift your right hand to your shoulder to repeat the rubbing procedure, drop the coin down your shirt collar.

**5**

Now show that the coin has disappeared.

**6**

## Effect

You borrow a coin and appear to make it pass through a solid table. This is a classic in magic circles, often being done with more than one coin.

| | | |
|---|---|---|
| Wow factor | ★ ★ ★ ★ ★ | |
| Performance skills | ★ ★ ★ ★ ★ | |
| Skill | ★ ★ ★ ★ ★ | |
| Time to learn | 1.5 hours | |
| Set up time | None needed | |

**1**

Ask to borrow a spectator's coin. Show it in your left hand, tap it on the table at various places and explain that this is a solid coin and a very solid table. Then mention every table has a soft spot. Show the coin, ready to do a French Drop (see page 16) – very smoothly, keeping the coin secretly in your right hand. Remember, don't move it too quickly.

**2**

As the right hand moves away pretending to hold the coin at its fingertips, allow your left hand to drop below the edge of table and position it underneath.

**3**

Pretend to tap the table with the coin in your right hand. As you do this, actually tap the table underneath with the coin. Rehearse getting the taps to match your hand tapping.

Wait for a second and slowly lift your right hand up to show the coin has vanished. Slowly bring the coin from underneath the table and display it in your outstretched hand.

**4**

Slap your hand flat on the table and, at the same time, slap underneath the table with your left hand. It will sound like the coin is under your right hand and on the table.

**5**

## Effect

A blank piece of paper is shown to the audience and then folded into eight. It is then unfolded, miraculously turning into a banknote. This effect needs some preparation before it is performed.

**1**

You will need a new banknote and a piece of paper of exactly the same size.

**2**

Fold the paper exactly in half along the middle, then along the middle again. Unfold and concertina. Turn the paper a half turn and fold it in half again. Unfold the paper and refold, this time bending the paper the other way. When this has been done, fold the paper in a concertina style from left to right.

**3**

Repeat this using the banknote, so that they are folded in the same way.

Put some paper glue on the top right corner of the paper.

**4**

Stick the corner of the paper to the lower right corner of the banknote. Make sure the edges match.

**5**

**6**

Fold the banknote along its creases so it is now folded neatly in the top right corner of the paper.

Turn over the paper and hold it so that the folded banknote is in your right fingers. This is how you hold the paper when you start the trick.

**7**

**8**

When presenting the trick, hold the paper with both hands, thumbs on top and fingers below. Show the paper, front and back, by turning your wrist.

| | |
|---|---|
| Wow factor | ★★★★★ |
| Performance skills | ★★★★★ |
| Skill | ★★★★★ |
| Time to learn | 1 hour |
| Set up time | 15 mins |

**9**

With the front of the paper to the audience, fold the paper, left to right along the creases, with your left hand. As you fold the last crease, turn the whole pad of paper over. Use a shake of the wrists to hide the movement.

**10**

Slowly unfold the note, using the right thumb to help. The left fingers take an edge and unfold the note. Turn your wrist to show the note on both sides. This time the paper is under the fingers on the right hand.

Fold the note and put it away.

**11**

## TOP TIP!
Have a spare note with creases in your pocket to pull out if people want to examine the money.

## PSYCHIC CAPS

Take three plastic milk bottle caps. Place a coin under one and turn your back, then the spectator messes them up but you can tell which cap the coin is under. Before you start the trick, use a small dab of glue and stick a hair on the coin so it sticks out from under the cap. When they have been mixed up look for the hair.

## NOTE FROM BOTTLE TRICK

This is a classic trick with a banknote and bottle. A glass bottle with a long neck, for example, a Cola bottle, works best. Place a note such as a $1 or £5 on the table then turn an empty Cola bottle upside down on top of it. The challenge is to get the note out from underneath the bottle without knocking over the bottle. You cannot touch the bottle, and it must remain upside down at all times. When no one can do it properly, show them. You roll up the note tightly until it pulls itself out from under the bottle.

## SWEET SLEEVES

Hold a small coin on your middle finger and then click your fingers and it will fly off. If you do this with your hand palm-down and wear a loose sleeve jacket, then the coin will shoot up your sleeve – a great way to make a coin disappear. To make it reappear, just lower your arm to your side and catch it when it falls out. This is the basis for what magicians call 'sleeving'.

## MESMERIZING MAGNETISM!

Hold a magnetic coin (available from magic stores) in your hand between your thumb and first and second fingers. Then push a small and flat magnet against the back of the coin with your thumb. Now get a second magnetic coin and hold it edge to edge against the first coin's lower edge. Slowly remove the hand holding it and it will hang there as if by magic! Having done this try and slowly spin the coin.

## VANISHING PENCIL AND COIN

With a coin in your left hand in front of you, say you are going to strike it three times with a pencil and make it vanish. Strike the coin twice with the pencil in your right hand, then bring the pencil up to your head for the third time. As you come up, put the pencil behind your ear. As you bring your hand down see the pencil is missing and point to your ear. As you point, turn your body toward the spectator, drop your left hand and put the coin in your pocket. As you take the pencil, close your left hand and strike it – wow, the coin has gone!

## VANISHING ACT

Many countries have copper coins and some of these are magnetic. If you find a magnetic coin, try having a magnet sewn into your sleeve – you can then make the coin 'disappear' by waving it over the sleeve.

## POCKETED!

Try holding a coin in the palm of your hand and tossing it up in the air and catching it a couple of times. As you do so, watch the coin go up and down – and be sure to follow it with your head. Then on the third or fourth time, pretend to throw it up (while secretly keeping it in your hand) and keep your head moving up and down as if watching the invisible coin. To the audience, it will look like the coin has vanished into thin air as you secretly slip the coin into your pocket.

## COIN FROM EAR

Here is a very simple way to perform one of the classics. To start you must have the coin you want to produce held lightly in the fingers of your right hand; curl the ends of your fingers slightly to hold the coin in place and hold your arm naturally by your side. Imagine seeing a coin in a person's ear and reach to take it, imagine you're going to pinch it with your thumb and first finger. As your hand goes to the side of their head, use your thumb to push the coin up into view. As you move your hand back, show them the coin.

# CHAPTER 3

Magic with everyday props which appears to happen spontaneously often has the strongest effect. This chapter presents a mixture of tricks; that need preparation and those that you can do off-the-cuff. The tricks are based on items you might find in a diner or café, whether a burger joint or a pizza restaurant. Objects needed include everyday items such as straws, napkins and spoons.

As ever, many of these effects need practice and, if they require setting up, it should be done beforehand. Once you are set up and ready to go, wait until the time is right. Don't rush into performing, try and catch people when they are off guard and it is more effective.

A lot of tricks in this chapter rely on good presentation. The technical skill required is often low, but for the effects to have impact there needs to be a lot of patter, or talking, and jokes. But, sometimes, less talking and more focus on what is happening can be just as powerful.

## Effect

You take a paper napkin and with a few twists turn it into a lovely rose. Although the 'roses' take a little practice, they are easy to make from any type of napkin, but colors such as red make the best impression.

| | |
|---|---|
| Wow factor | ★★★★★ |
| Performance skills | ★★★★★ |
| Skill | ★★★★★ |
| Time to learn | 1 hour |
| Set up time | None needed |

**1** Open the layer of the napkin out and fold the top edge down about 2in/5cm. Catch the fold between the index and middle finger, approximately 1in/2.5cm from the end. Wrap the napkin around the index and middle finger so that the folded-down portion stays on the inside.

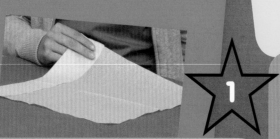

**2** Keep wrapping the napkin around the index and middle fingers until it is completely wrapped around them. Wrap securely but not too tightly, because in step three you will remove the napkin from the fingers to complete the rose.

**3** Now, pinch the napkin together with your other hand. While the two fingers are still in the napkin, give the spot at which you have pinched the napkin a firm twist or two. You can remove the fingers from the wrapped napkin at this point. Continue to twist the napkin downward from the point at which you pinched below the twist. Twist firmly and evenly to about halfway down the lower portion.

**4** Hold the twist securely with one hand and, with the other find the lower outside corner of the napkin. Work the corner loose, and gently pull it up to the twisted portion to form a leaf. Pinch securely at the leaf and continue to twist the remainder of the napkin firmly.

**5** Hold the 'rose' securely at the base where the flower joins the twisted stem. Reach into the center of the flower and pinch it with two fingers. Give a twist in the direction of the turns, enhancing the center of the rose.

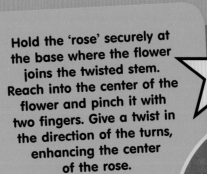

**TOP TIP!**
Napkins come in two or three ply and the rose works best with one ply – so remember to separate them first!

## Effect

You take a paper napkin and ask a spectator to copy you. As you screw it up into your hand and do a magic wave, yours has shrunk in size whereas the spectator's hasn't. This is a great trick to do alongside the Napkin To Rose (opposite page) and always draws a laugh because the spectator can't do it.

| Wow factor | ★★★★★ |
|---|---|
| Performance skills | ★★★★★ |
| Skill | ★★★★★ |
| Time to learn | 30 minutes |
| Set up time | None needed |

**1** Have a spectator copy your actions. Open a single layer of the napkin out and hold it from one corner, with your first finger and thumb. Leave about 1in/2.5cm sticking out above them.

**2** Start wrapping the napkin up and pushing it into your fist.

**3** As you do this, secretly tear the napkin below your finger and thumb. Make sure nobody notices.

Slowly push the top of the napkin into your fist and make a magic wave. Now start to rub your fingers and open your hand as you show a small ball of napkin.

**4** As you push the napkin into your fist, show everyone the napkin inside your hand.

Secretly steal the torn napkin out of your left hand using your right thumb. As you do this, move your left hand forward and show the napkin sticking out from the top.

**5**

**TOP TIP!**
It is important you keep showing the spectator the napkin and get them to push theirs in nice and tight. This takes the attention away from what you are doing.

## Effect

This is a trick to impress your friends and family. It's simple and, if done properly, always effective.

| Wow factor | ★★★★★ |
|---|---|
| Performance skills | ★★★★★ |
| Skill | ★★★★★ |
| Time to learn | 45 minutes |
| Set up time | None needed |

**1**
Take a cocktail napkin and fold it until it is about the size of a 50 cent piece or a £2 coin. Take a second cocktail napkin and place it on top of the folded-up napkin on a table.

**2**
Put the folded napkin somewhere that you can pick up both napkins without letting anyone know that you have a folded napkin underneath. A good place is in the right-hand corner nearest to you. Pick up the napkins, keeping the folded one towards you.

**3**
Now carefully shred the unfolded napkin until it is a lump of shredded paper roughly the same size as the folded-up one. After the last tear, pretend to be fussing over the condition of the paper. Maybe adjust a couple of pieces or fold one piece over.

**4**
As you fuss with the napkin, flip the paper over so that the folded piece is facing the spectators and the ripped piece is facing you.

**5**
Unfold the paper slowly. When the paper is big enough to hide the movement – a third or a half unfolded – sneak the ripped-up paper into your fingers. Finish opening the paper and hand it to a spectator.

**6**
Casually put the wad of paper into your pocket while the spectators are looking at the 'restored' napkin. If you are sitting at a table, maybe throw it under the table.

## Effect

A spoon appears to be bent in half and straightened again. It can be done with a fork or a knife and doesn't even need the coin, as described here, to work. It is a very good optical illusion – but don't overuse it.

| | |
|---|---|
| Wow factor | ★★★ ★ ★ |
| Performance skills | ★★★★ ★ |
| Skill | ★★★ ★ ★ |
| Time to learn | 30 minutes |
| Set up time | None needed |

**1**

Hold a spoon and a coin in each hand.

**2**

Position the tip of the spoon against a table. You should have your fingers in front of the handle – except your ring (third) finger, which goes behind. Your thumb should be near the top of the spoon. Hold a coin between it and the first finger. Use the top of the coin, to make it look like the top of the spoon. The left hand wraps around the right hand, thumb to thumb.

**3**

Roll the spoon against the table and keep the hands straight up, though allow the spoon to rotate between the fingers.

From the front, with both hands hiding the method, the illusion works.

**4**

Straighten the spoon by allowing it to roll back up, as if it is made of rubber unbending itself.

**5**

# Effect

A straw magically appears between your fingertips.

| Wow factor | ★ ★ ★ ★ ★ |
|---|---|
| Performance skills | ★ ★ ★ ★ ★ |
| Skill | ★ ★ ★ ★ ★ |
| Time to learn | 45 minutes |
| Set up time | 5 minutes |

**1** Before you do this trick you need a straw, preferably with stripes. Cut it along one side.

**2** Roll the straw up along its length so it is a small tube.

**3** Use a paper clip to hold it in place. Put this in your pocket and you are ready to go.

**4** In front of an audience, secretly take the rolled-up straw out of your pocket, removing the paper clip, and hold it in your fingers. Your fingers keep the straw rolled up. This is called a finger palm position.

**5** Look into the air - imagine you can see the straw – and reach up with your right hand, fingers to the audience. Bring your left hand up so the fingers touch, and slightly overlap.

**6** Use your left thumb to start to unroll the straw as you pull your fingers apart, and the straw appears.

★ **TOP TIP!** Don't try to drink with the straw – it won't work!

## Effect

You have three straws in your hand. When you remove one, you still have three straws in your hand! Repeat this effect three times.

| Wow factor | ⭐ ⭐ ⭐ ⭐ ⭐ |
|---|---|
| Performance skills | ⭐ ⭐ ⭐ ⭐ ⭐ |
| Skill | ⭐ ⭐ ⭐ ⭐ |
| Time to learn | 1 hour |
| Set up time | 10 minutes |

**1**

You will need six straws, preferably with stripes. Prepare three straws by cutting them from end to end. Then fit one of these straws over each of the uncut straws, leaving about 1in/2.5 cm over the end for you to grab hold of.

**2**

Hold three straws in your right hand, with the side splits towards you. Count them to the audience.

**3**

Take hold of the top of one of the straws with your right hand, then, while holding on to the bottom with your left hand, pull it off in one smooth action.

**4**

It should look like you have taken a straw but still have three left. Do this again, twice.

**TOP TIP!**

As you take the straw you should look at it, this will focus the audience's attention on that. Then do a double-take at the three straws still left.

# Effect

The magician takes two plastic drinking straws and wraps them around each other. They appear to be tightly interlocked, but a quick pull separates them completely.

| | |
|---|---|
| Wow factor | ★★★★★ |
| Performance skills | ★★★★★ |
| Skill | ★★★★★ |
| Time to learn | 2 hours |
| Set up time | None needed |

**1**

Hold the two straws crossed at the center, with the horizontal one in front of the vertical one.

**2**

Bring the lower part of the vertical straw forward across the horizontal straw. Now bring the bottom part of the vertical straw up behind the horizontal straw so it appears to be a fully wrapped around the other.

**4**

Take both ends of the vertical straw, pull them to the right, and then pull the straws apart with a quick snap.

**3**

Take the right half of the horizontal straw and give it a full wrap behind the top part of the vertical straw. Continue another half wrap so that both ends are on the left side.

## TOP TIP!

This is a very visual trick and works well with two straws of contrasting colors. It can also be done using balloons.

# Effect

Astound your audience by swinging a bottle like a pendulum with only an untied piece of rope coming out of the end.

| Wow factor | ★ ★ ★ ★ |
|---|---|
| Performance skills | ★ ★ ★ ★ ★ |
| Skill | ★ ★ ★ ★ |
| Time to learn | 30 minutes |
| Set up time | None needed |

**1**

You need a piece of rope and a small enough ball of cork for the bottle you choose. For safety reasons a plastic one is ideal

**2**

Push the cork ball inside the bottle before you invite the audience to come and watch your trick.

**3**

Now show the audience the bottle and the rope. Make sure that you're ready to go!

**4**

Push the end of the rope into the bottle slowly. As you do this, you must turn the bottle upside down and let the cork ball lodge between the rope and the neck of the bottle. Gently tug on the rope to confirm that the ball is wedged and the rope won't fall out.

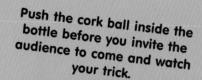

**5**

Now slowly begin to swing the bottle backwards and forwards as you would a pendulum.

**6**

Stop swinging the bottle and, for the finishing touch, hold the bottle upside down and show the audience that the rope doesn't fall out – it defies gravity! Turn the bottle the right way up and pull the rope out. Then show the audience the bottom of the bottle so they can see for themselves. As you do this, let the cork ball slip out of the end and out of view into your hand.

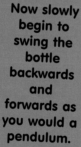

# DINNER MEDLEY

## FOUR CORNERS

Four cherry stones or raisins are placed in the middle of a small saucer. The challenge is to move them to the outside in four different places without touching them. The answer is simple: spin the plate and the centrifugal force will push them to the outside edges.

## PREDICTA CUBE

All you need is some sugar cubes and a pencil – a soft 'B' pencil is best – for this great trick. You ask someone to choose a number and write it on one side of the cube. You then dissolve the sugar in a drink – water, tea, coffee – and read the top of the drink to tell them their number. The trick is, as you take the cube between your thumb and finger, make sure the side with the writing on presses against your finger or thumb and it will leave an impression of the number for you to read.

## A STRAW CHALLENGE

Give your friend an empty plastic bottle – the heavier the bottle the better the stunt – and a straw. Ask them to pick up the bottle using one hand and the straw. When they have tried a few times, show them the secret. You bend the straw and push the bend into the neck. Let the straw open a little as the bottle gets wider, then pull it up so it jams. Then pick it up.

## BOUNCING BREAD

At dinner, you pick up a bread roll and appear to bounce it on the floor. Hold a bread roll in your right hand, about shoulder height. Pretend to bounce it on the floor but, as your hand goes below the table, keep hold of the roll and stamp your foot as if it has hit the floor. Then throw the roll up in the air from under the table. This requires practice and timing for the best effect.

## PSYCHIC STRAW

You appear to make a straw or pencil move by thought alone. You place a straw or pencil on the table and then hold out your right hand and extend your first finger. You slowly point the finger towards the straw and it slowly rolls forward without touching it. The trick is to slowly blow along your arm, not too hard but soft and gently. Then the straw or pencil will move.

## SALT CELLAR THRU TABLE

Try covering a salt cellar with a napkin, banging the table a little with it, holding it in your right hand. Then relax as you sit back, move your hand to the edge of the table and let the cellar drop into your lap (but don't let people see this). Keeping the napkin in the same shape, lean forward and smash the napkin into the table. As you do this, reach under the table with your left hand and pick up the salt cellar and reveal.

## COOKIES

Small packets of cookies can be great for jokes, such as making them vanish by eating them! Try some of the coin tricks and moves out with small cookies – they work really well.

## STRAW POPPING

Take a straw and squeeze the ends shut. Hold an end in each hand and roll your hands forward, wrapping up the ends of the straw. When the straw is about 2in/5cm or less, get a friend to flick it hard with their fingers. It will make a great bang or popping sound. This is not a trick but still lots of fun!

# CHAPTER 4

Playing cards have been around for thousands of years; used across many cultures to play games, gamble and predict the future.

Originally, cards were round and hand painted, making them very expensive. Often, they were only used by royalty, who had their faces painted on the cards that became known as 'Kings' and 'Queens'. These in turn became the picture cards we have today.

Cards are used for thousands of tricks: the basic one is when a person thinks of a card and the magician finds it. The harder the way the card is found or the more impossible the location it is found in, and the more dramatic the revelation, the better the trick. Magician David Blaine threw cards at a car and the chosen card was actually inside the car's windshield!

Cards are used by magicians on stage, who manipulate them, creating patterns and fans and making cards appear and vanish at their fingertips.

Card tricks are often the first type of magic we encounter. When done well, they amuse and amaze. When done badly, they can become very boring. This chapter has self-working tricks, a few basic flourishes, basic card techniques and great tricks to learn, but it is only a small taster to start you off as a card magician.

## Effect

A 'force' is a way to get your audience member to take a specific card. However, it must seem as if they have made a free choice. In this case, when you write a prediction, and the spectator cuts to a card, the magician's prediction matches the card. Or you can force any card on to the spectator and then use your imagination to create your own incredible ending!

As you shuffle the deck, glimpse the bottom card (For example, Jack of Clubs). Set the deck down in front of the spectator. Write down the card you saw on the bottom as the prediction.

| | |
|---|---|
| Wow factor | ★ ★ ★ ★ ★ |
| Performance skills | ★ ★ ★ ★ ★ |
| Skill | ★ ★ ★ ★ ★ |
| Time to learn | 15 minutes |
| Set up time | None needed |

**1** Tell the spectator to cut the deck in half. Have them set the top half next to the bottom half. Pick up the bottom half and place it on top of the top half, but rotated 90 degrees. Say that you are 'marking the cut'.

**2** Now here is the hardest part. Look them in the eye and wait for eye contact. You must get them to look away from the deck so they forget which pile is which. Point to the prediction to remind them that you have predicted that they will cut to a specific card. Time is on your side. You need to pause for a few moments, just long enough for them to forget which pile is which.

**3** Now pick up the top half of the deck (previously the bottom half) and turn it face up.

**4** Take a step back. Point to that card. Say, "You chose the Jack of Clubs." Now turn to the spectator and have them pick up the prediction... and of course it matches!

CARD FORCE 2 – SLIP FORCE

## Effect

The slip force is a harder force to master than the X-Cut but it is more deceptive. It is simple but very effective when done well. The magician runs his or her thumb down the side of the cards, the spectator says 'stop' and then takes the top card at their chosen spot.

| Wow factor | ★★★★★ |
|---|---|
| Performance skills | ★★★★★ |
| Skill | ★★★★★ |
| Time to learn | 45 minutes |
| Set up time | None needed |

**1**

Start with the card to be forced on top of the deck. For ease we have marked it with a cross in the pictures.

**2**

Hold the deck in a mechanic's grip (see below). Bend your first finger under the deck and run your thumb down the corner of the cards. Ask the spectator to say 'stop' as you riffle down the cards.

**3**

The right hand picks up the top block of 'riffled cards' from above. This pack is lifted straight up. As you do this...

**4**

... your fingers in the left hand exert pressure on the top card (the forced card) so it slides or falls flush with the deck underneath and becomes the top card of the lower half of the deck.

**5**

This may make a noise, or 'talk', so tap the long edge of the half in your right hand on the deck to straighten the cards. This adds cover to the move and disguises the noise. Extend your right arm and have the spectator take the 'freely' chosen card.

### TOP TIP!

This force needs to be performed casually; any tension in your hands or body will tell people you are doing something fishy. Relax and don't look at your hands as you do this move.

## Effect

As you dribble the cards from one hand to the other, the spectator says 'stop', returns their card to the deck and you dribble the rest of the cards. Then you cut the deck and their chosen card is on the top of the deck.

| Wow factor | ★★★★★ |
|---|---|
| Performance skills | ★★★★★ |
| Skill | ★★★★★ |
| Time to learn | 1 hour |
| Set up time | None needed |

**1** After a card is selected the spectator removes the card. You then dribble the cards from your right hand to your left. The spectator says 'stop'. You square up the pile in your left hand.

**2** The spectator places their card on the pile in your left hand and you continue to dribble the rest of the deck on to your hand. Make sure you dribble the first few cards towards you, so they stick out at the back of the pack.

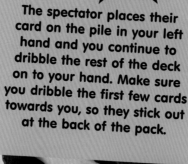

**3** As you square up the deck with the right hand, your right thumb lifts the top cards up a bit and creates a break above the spectator's selected card as you pick up the deck.

**4** Cut off the cards above the break, and place hard on a table.

**5** Drop the bottom of the deck back.

**6** The selected card should now be on the top of the deck.

**Extra Trick!**
You can have the spectator's card signed to add to the effect.

**TOP TIP!**
This needs to be relaxed and flowing so must be practiced hard.

# Effect

This sleight of hand allows you to have a card on the bottom of the deck you are holding and appear to place it on the table but still leave the card on the bottom of the deck.

| Wow factor | ★ ★ ★ ★ ★ |
|---|---|
| Performance skills | ★ ★ ★ ★ ★ |
| Skill | ★ ★ ★ ★ ★ |
| Time to learn | 1 hour |
| Set up time | None needed |

## 1

Hold the pack face up in the left hand between the first joint of the thumb on one side and the second joints of the four fingers on the other.

## 2

Do not call attention to the bottom card. Turn the pack face downwards and, with the tip of the left finger, draw the bottom card back towards the body about 3/4in/2cm.

## 3

Now, with the tip of the right hand second finger, draw out the next card, and put it face downwards on the table.

### Extra Trick!

This method of doing the Glide involves wrapping the fingers around the end of the deck and removing cards from the opposite end. There is another way: hold the deck by your finger tips, with three fingers along one side, your little finger at the rear of the deck and your thumb across from the three fingers. Now, using the fleshy part of the middle finger of your other hand, push the bottom card back against your little finger, then tip your middle finger up slightly and draw out the next card. When this card is clear of the deck, so it can be taken by your fingers, put the bottom card back by pressing it into place with the little finger of the hand holding the deck.

## Effect

This sleight allows you to apparently show the top card but in fact you turn two cards over as one.

| Wow factor | ★ ★ ★ ★ ★ |
| --- | --- |
| Performance skills | ★ ★ ★ ★ ★ |
| Skill | ★ ★ ★ ★ ★ |
| Time to learn | 2 hours |
| Set up time | None needed |

**1** Square the pack in the left hand face down and bring the right hand over it, thumb at the rear, fingers on the outer end. Make a motion of squaring the ends and, at the same time, press the fingers back a little making the ends of the deck slightly wedge-shaped.

**2** With the ball of the thumb, lift the rear ends of the two top cards and slip the tip of the left little finger under them. This is called 'taking a break'.

**3** With the right thumb tip on the back of the two cards and the tip of the right forefinger on the face, turn the two cards as one and lay them face up on top of the pack, the ends protruding over the inner end of the deck for about 1/2in/1cm. Exhibit the card in this position, name it out loud then seize the cards again at the lower outer corner as before and turn them face down on the back of the pack.

### Extra Trick!

Shuffle the deck and double lift to show the second card's face (say, the Queen of Hearts). Place both cards back on the deck and take off the top card holding it face down. Say, "If I really don't want the Queen of Hearts, I can simply change it for one I want by rubbing the spots through the deck."

When you say this, put the card part way into the deck and rub it a bit before you remove it and show its face. Now it has changed into another card (For example, the Seven of Clubs). While they look at the card in surprise, cut or shuffle the deck. The cards given are examples.

### This is the hard bit

If you do a double lift, try holding the two cards as one with your thumb on the bottom right corner and your index finger on the top left and spin the card before putting it back on the deck. This flourish makes it look like one card – it is what is know as a convincer. Be careful the cards don't split and show two cards.

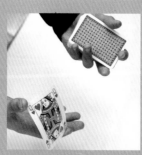

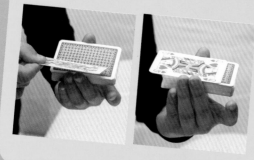

## Effect

The Riffle Shuffle is used by many card dealers in casinos. It shows youcan really handle a pack of cards.

| | | |
|---|---|---|
| Wow factor | ★★★★★ | |
| Performance skills | ★★★★★ | |
| Skill | ★★★★★ | |
| Time to learn | 1 hour | |
| Set up time | None needed | |

**1**
Cut the deck into two halves, placing them on the table with the two short edges facing each other. Pick up the cards and hold them.

**2**
To begin the riffle, start by bending the cards towards the air and move the decks in close, so when you let go they contact each other.

Now put your thumbs on the back of the cards and use your fingers to push the cards up from underneath. Release pressure with your fingers and the cards should have enough room to just fall into your fingers.

**3**

**4**
After they have fallen into your hand, just square off the deck and it is shuffled.

### TOP TIP!
Once mastered, the riffle shuffle can be done in the hands and finished with a nice waterfall of cards (this is done by keeping one hand lower and letting the cards flow from one hand to the other). If you handle the deck of cards well, you'll impress your audience before you even start.

# Effect

This is what is known as the 'self-working' effect that relies on presentation and was popularized by the magician Karl Fulves although the original idea was by Dr John Hammond. It can be performed with a pack of cards in any condition.

| | |
|---|---|
| Wow factor | ★★★★★ |
| Performance skills | ★★★★★ |
| Skill | ★★★★★ |
| Time to learn | 60 minutes |
| Set up time | 1 minute |

**★2**

Ask the spectator to shuffle the cards. As you take the deck, make a mental note of the top and bottom card. This can be done when showing the spectator the cards are truly shuffled. In this example, they are the King of Hearts on top and the Ace of Spades on the bottom.

Take two 'prediction' cards out of the pack. The prediction cards are actually the twins (the twin is the same value in the other suit of the same color) of the top and bottom cards of the deck. Remove the prediction cards and place them face up on the table. Say their names and color, for example, the black Ace of Clubs and the red King of Diamonds.

Instruct the spectator to deal cards into a pile face down and stop whenever they wish, with a card in their hand – offer them the choice of the card on the table, in their hand or on the deck. Place the chosen card on the pile.

**★3**

**★6**

Run through the deck to find that the card to the right of each face-up card is their twin.

**★1**

Place the twin of the card originally on the bottom of the deck onto the dealt pile face up with their chosen card, in this case the Ace of Clubs. The spectator will then place the rest of the deck on top of the face-up card.

Get the spectator to gather the deck and repeat dealing. When they stop, place the other face-up card (King of Diamonds) at that point and get them to put the deck on top of that.

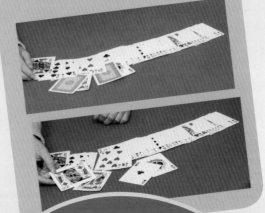

**★4**

**★5**

## TOP TIP!
When performing this you can build a story around the idea of cards having a twin. Also remember to mention that the twin card is one with the same value in the opposite suit – Hearts and Diamonds, Spades and Clubs. You may prefer to count the cards yourself if you have an awkward spectator!

# Effect

This is a famous card trick created by Paul Curry around 1942. The spectator 'guesses' the color of the suit of each card in the deck, and gets 100 percent right! But it's is very simple: the deck used by the magician is stacked, with all the black cards at the top and all the red cards at the bottom.

| Wow factor | ★ ★ ★ ★ ★ |
|---|---|
| Performance skills | ★ ★ ★ ★ ★ |
| Skill | ★ ★ ★ ★ ★ |
| Time to learn | 1.5 hours |
| Set up time | 5 minutes |

**1** Take the stacked deck of cards and place on the table two face-up cards known as 'markers', one black and one red – the black on the left and the red on the right. Tell the spectator that they are going to deal cards face down from the deck and that the aim is for them to use the power of their mind to identify whether each card in the deck is black or red.

**2** Take one card at a time from the deck, face down, and ask the spectator to tell whether it is black or red. You then place the card in line with the appropriately colored marker card, overlapping it at the bottom.

About halfway through the deck, stop and tell the spectator that it is necessary to switch sides in order to prevent a possible preference for one side over another.

**3** Then deal two new marker cards on to the existing lines: a red one on the left, and a black one on the right.

The exposed lines reveal that every one of the spectator's guesses was correct, and the black and red cards have been exactly sorted by color.

**4** Continue as before, dealing cards face down from the deck on to the spectator's choice of the black or red line.

When the deck is finished, instruct the spectator to gather up and somehow reveal the left-hand line of cards.

**5** Do the same for the right-hand line. As you do, either move the red marker card from one end of the line to the other, or reverse the order of all other cards in the line. You must perform this during the act of gathering up the right-hand line of cards, while the spectator is distracted by gathering up their own line. Since the cards are gathered into a stack at that point, this is fairly easy.

**TOP TIP!** This is an excellent trick to perform but you must set the deck up and wait a while to build anticipation.

# Effect

The four Jacks act as robbers who successfully rob a bank (the deck) and make a miraculous getaway. Each Jack goes into a different place in the deck and, as the police come, they all rise to the top and get away. This is a great beginner's card trick.

★ 1

First, prepare for the trick by removing the four Jacks, as well as three random cards from the deck of cards. Position the four Jacks fanned out in your right hand with the three random cards behind the last Jack.

★ 2

To your audience, this should look like only four Jacks. In this photo, the random cards are behind the Jack of Clubs.

★ 4

"The first Jack went to the basement and broke into the safe and stole all the jewels." Take the top random card and slide it into the deck near the bottom. Don't let the audience actually see this card. Try and do it naturally.

★ 3

As you show the Jacks, say, "Let me tell you a little story about how the four Jacks' robbed a bank. When the bank was closed, in the dead of night they parachuted on to the roof of the bank." Place all seven cards (the four Jacks, and on top of those the three random cards) on the top of the face-down deck. It should look like you have placed four Jacks on top of the deck. Do this casually.

| Wow factor | ★ ★ ★ ★ ★ |
|---|---|
| Performance skills | ★ ★ ★ ★ ★ |
| Skill | ★ ★ ★ ★ ★ |
| Time to learn | 1 hour |
| Set up time | 1 minute |

**5** "The second Jack abseiled down the building to the first floor where they kept the money, went in the window and stole it." Take the next card (the one on top of the deck) and put it into the middle of the deck.

**8** Excitedly say, "Then the police came! Lucky for the Jacks, the last Jack had a whistle and blew it as he jumped up and down on the roof." As you say this, take the top Jack, pick it up and have it jump about.

**6** "The third Jack went to the top floor and stole all the gold." Place the third random card near the top of the deck.

**7** "The last Jack stayed on the roof and kept an eye out for the police." Pick up the last Jack and casually flash the face to the audience. Make it look like this wasn't deliberate, and show it briefly so that they barely see it. We are trying to create the impression that you showed them all the other Jacks when they replay this trick in their mind later.

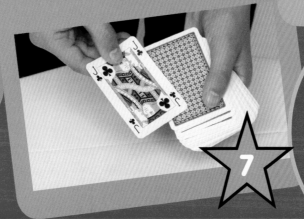

## TOP TIP!
Once you are happy with the methods you can develop your own story. It is the story that adds to the enjoyment of this effect. If you interest people with the story they are more impressed with the effect.

**9** "All the Jacks rushed to the top and escaped into their helicopter." As you do this, one by one flip over the Jacks on the top of the deck or throw them on to the table face up. It looks cooler if you can do this and make them spin a little as they land, creating a helicopter effect.

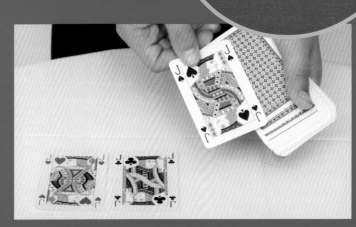

## Effect

This is similar to an effect performed by David Blaine. This version requires you to force a card and requires some set-up. Do it outside, ideally on a football or baseball pitch or near some earth which is warm and even slightly wet. The name of a spectator's card is revealed in earth on your arm.

| Wow factor | ★ ★ ★ ★ ★ |
|---|---|
| Performance skills | ★ ★ ★ ★ ★ |
| Skill | ★ ★ ★ ★ ★ |
| Time to learn | 1 hour |
| Set up time | 1 minute |

## Preparation

Before you start, decide on which card you are going to force, for example, Four of Hearts. Then take a bar of soap and ensure it has corners on it. Write the name of the card on your forearm with the soap. Here, we use the 4♥.

**1** Force the card on the spectator using your favorite method. Get them to remember the card and return it to the deck.

**2** Ask the spectator to write the name of their card in earth on the floor and then rub it out.

**3** Explain you have special powers that allow you to read thoughts from the ground as you are in touch with nature. Collect some earth and rub it in your hands – to warm it up as if it is dry.

**4** Rub it on your forearm where the soap writing is (invisible at present). As you rub it in, the card name is revealed.

**5** The name of the card will be written in the earth if it is dry. If it is wet, it will run off the wax and be clear with the earth around it.

**TOP TIP!**
This is a great way to reveal a card but can be used with a bit of imagination to reveal all sorts of information. This trick works well when performed with the right dramatic effect.

**Extra Trick!**
You can use paper glue instead of soap. If you do, it will leave your arm tacky but it does allow use of all sorts of other items such as glitter, talcum powder, flour or salt to reveal the card.

## Effect

The spectator cuts the deck into four piles. From each pile, three random cards are dealt on to each of the other piles. The top card of each pile is turned over to reveal all four Aces.

| | | |
|---|---|---|
| Wow factor | ★★★★★ | |
| Performance skills | ★★★★★ | |
| Skill | ★★★★★ | |
| Time to learn | 1 hour | |
| Set up time | None needed | |

**2**

**3**

**1**

Before you start, secretly put all four Aces face down on to the top of the deck.

Hand the deck to a spectator, and ask them to cut the deck into two halves. Once they have done that, have them divide each of the two piles into half, leaving you with four piles. Remember where the top of the original deck is. We will call the piles numbers one to four, four being the top pile with the Aces. (Don't tell the spectator these numbers. They are just for us to keep track of things.)

Have the spectator pick up pile one, put the top three cards on to the bottom, and deal the (now) top three cards one to each of the other piles (two, three, and four, one card to each pile).

**4**

The spectator continues, in order, to do the same with the other piles. (You just point to each pile, when you want them to use it.) Make sure the pile with the Aces is last.

Once this has been done, recap events to the spectator and cut the deck into four, and randomly move cards about.

Ask the spectator if it would be coincidence, freaky or just magic if all the top cards were Aces. As you are doing this, turn over the top cards to reveal the Aces.

**5**

**6**

## Effect

Once you have either forced a card (see page 34) or had a card chosen and returned to the pack, and controlled, the next stage is to to reveal it. Some revelations can be very quick. Others need building up to.

If you can force a card – or have a card selected – and have five ways of revealing a card, you have five tricks. If you have two ways of getting a card chosen with five ways of revealing the card you then have ten tricks. It's that simple.

Here we consider four types of revelation: Say It, Text It, A Pressure Turnover and The Leg Reverse.

### Revelation 1 – Say It

You know the card chosen – let's say it's the Three of Clubs.

Say to the spectator: "Please think of your card and concentrate on it hard. Keep repeating the name to yourself in your head, concentrate on the card's name, keep saying its name, like a mantra, keep repeating it, over and over – for instance, the Three of Clubs, the Three of Clubs, the Three of Clubs..."

### Revelation 2 – Text it

You have forced the card chosen – let's say it's the Five of Diamonds.

This needs some preparation but use your cell phone and have a prediction, on a text saying you chose the Five of Diamonds or have a photo of you holding the card or even a small video clip.

When your spectator has chosen the forced card and returned it to the deck, get them to shuffle the cards. Ask them for their mobile number and say you are going to use your phone to find their card. Have them place their phone (switched on) on the shuffled deck. As they do that, send the text, photo or video. When the phone beeps, ask them to look at what it says.

### Revelation 3 – A Pressure Turnover

## Effect

Here the chosen card appears to jump out and on top of the deck face up. This requires a lot of practice. A card is freely chosen and signed and returned to the deck and controlled to the top. You can do this using the In-Jog from page 36. Say you are going to make the card jump out of the deck and do three and a half somersaults and land on top of the deck.

**1** Hold the deck in the right hand, in an over grip with the fingers and thumbs on opposite sides, fingers furthest from the body.

**2** Push off the top card to the side under the palm of the hand, about 1in/3cm.

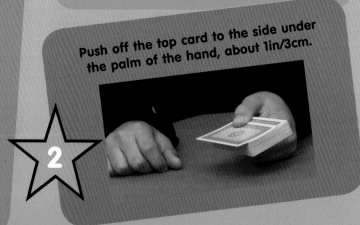

**3**

Drop the deck on to a table or hard surface, from about 16in/40cm. As you let go, jerk your right hand up. This is a knack and you only get a feel for it with some practice.

The top card separates from the deck, turns over and lands face up on the deck.

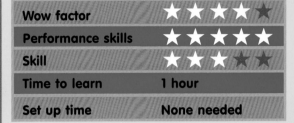

| Wow factor | ★ ★ ★ ★ ★ |
|---|---|
| Performance skills | ★ ★ ★ ★ ★ |
| Skill | ★ ★ ★ ★ ★ |
| Time to learn | 1 hour |
| Set up time | None needed |

**4**

### TOP TIP!
You can throw the cards to your left hand but that is harder still. However, it is more impressive – as is getting the card signed.

## Revelation 4 – The Leg Reverse

Making a card the only one face up in a face-down deck can be a great revelation. There are many ways to achieve this effect: this is one of them but requires good misdirection. Once again a card is freely chosen and signed and returned to the deck and controlled to the top. Again, do this using the In-Jog method.

| Wow factor | ★ ★ ★ ★ ★ |
|---|---|
| Performance skills | ★ ★ ★ ★ ★ |
| Skill | ★ ★ ★ ★ ★ |
| Time to learn | 1 hour |
| Set up time | None needed |

The chosen card is now on top of the deck. Hold the deck in your right hand.

Let the arm drop by your side. With your right thumb, push the top card to the right about a half inch/1cm.

**3**

Using your right thigh as a surface, turn this card face up on the deck.

Bring the cards up and casually cut them so the card is now face up in the deck.

**4**

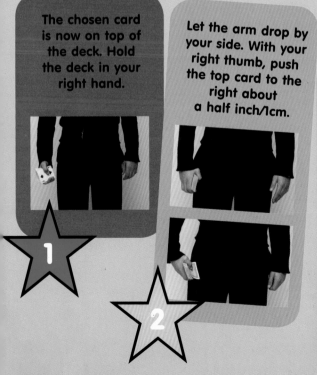

**1**

**2**

**5**

Spread cards for the revelation.

## Effect

The spectator is shown four Aces. The two black Aces are placed on their hand one at a time. They then instantly change into the two red Aces – and it is the magician who is now holding the two black Aces.

| Wow factor | ★★★★★ |
|---|---|
| Performance skills | ★★★★★ |
| Skill | ★★★★★ |
| Time to learn | 1.5 hours |
| Set up time | None needed |

**1** Use the Glide and the Double Lift moves from pages 37 and 38 for this trick. From a pack of cards, remove four Aces. Show them to the spectator in the shape of a fan.

**2** Take the Aces out of the deck and arrange them face up – Be sure that the Ace of Spades is on top. This is done casually as if you were playing with the cards.

**3** Turn the cards face down, use a glide to pull back the Ace of Spades and place the Ace of Diamonds on the table – but call it as the Ace of Spades.

**4** Set up for a double lift with a break under the top two cards.

**5** Double lift the top two cards to show the Ace of Clubs and then place the cards back on the pack.

**6** Place the top card on the table, calling it the Ace of Clubs.

**7** Snap fingers and show that the cards have changed place. Reveal you have the two black Aces.

**TOP TIP!** Watch out for spectators who want to grab the cards or turn the Aces over too early. If you tell them a joke while you perform, it helps prevent them from spoiling the trick.

## SHOOTING CARDS

Try shooting cards out of the deck by holding it in your right hand, in a dealer's grip with your hand underneath. Use your thumb to pull the top card down about a half in/ 1cm so it is protruding off the bottom edge. Now use your little finger to bend the card: by pushing your little finger towards the base of your thumb, the top card will spin out. It takes practice – try not to catch the card on your fingers as it spins. When you are more confident, shoot the card in the air and catch it with your other hand.

## AMBITIOUS CARD

Have a card selected and controlled to the top of the deck. Then place a card on top of it. Show the top card, replace it on the deck, do a double lift and show the chosen card is now on top. Put the top card in the deck, and the selected card is on top again!

Here's another version: instead of putting the top card in the deck, put it on the table under a glass, and do a Pressure Turnover revelation (see page 46) – so the chosen card has now jumped into the deck and turned itself over.

## COUNT DOWN

Have a card selected and control it to the bottom of the deck. Ask the spectator to name a number between 1 and 26, then, as you count from the bottom of the deck, using a Glide, the chosen card is now at the chosen number!

## THE LUCKY SEVENS

### Set-up

Place the four sevens on the top of your deck of cards. Ensure you have a pen or pencil and a piece of paper.

Now take the four sevens from the top of the deck of cards and lay them face down in a pile in front of the spectator. Now remove seven cards from the deck and put these cards in a separate pile. Tell the spectator that you read minds and will tell them which pile they will choose. Make a prediction (For example, "You picked the seven pile.") on your piece of paper and fold it and put it right alongside the cards. Now ask the spectator to choose one of the piles and then read the paper. No matter which is chosen, the note is correct. One pile contains the four sevens and the other pile contains seven cards. After the trick is finished put both piles on top of the deck. Note: try not to let them see both of the piles.

# CHAPTER 5

This chapter uses everyday items as props including rubber bands, ropes and string or thread.

Some of the effects are simple jokes, whereas others are full tricks which are used by many professional magicians. The moves and routines may only take a few hours to learn – but mastering them and presenting them well may take longer.

The performance of these effects takes many forms. One of these tricks – Tangled Thread (also known as The Hindu Thread) – is used by the great American magician Eugene Burger. He does it close up for a few people and on stage for thousands. Eugene has more than eight different stories and presentations for this one trick. Each presentation is unique to him and his audiences...and so should yours be too.

This chapter details pure magic that, once mastered, will last you a lifetime and be great to impress your friends and family.

However, remember that the trick is only the start. You have to make the trick into a performance that people are intrigued by and one that they want to watch. When putting together your presentations, write them down or record them and then see how they can be improved. Are they too wordy or too short, or maybe they don't match your personality?

## Effect

Make a rubber band jump from two fingers to two other fingers on the same hand. You put a rubber band around the bottom of your index and middle fingers. Show the audience the back of your hand. Now close your fist and say some magic words, swirling your other hand around your closed fist. Now open your hand and the rubber band jumps to your little and ring finger. For this you need an rubber band which is the right size for your hand. It needs to be able to hang loosely around two fingers.

| Wow factor | ⭐⭐⭐☆☆ |
| --- | --- |
| Performance skills | ⭐⭐⭐☆☆ |
| Skill | ⭐⭐☆☆☆ |
| Time to learn | 30 minutes |
| Set up time | None needed |

**1** Use an average-sized rubber band of regular elasticity. Put the rubber band over your first and middle fingers. Pull it all the way down to your knuckles. With your palm facing upwards, pull the rubber band out and toward your little finger. This lifting of the rubber band is proof that it really is on the two fingers. In fact this is where the secret move takes place. Three things occur at one and the same time.

**2** Bend all four fingers and put the ends of all of them in the rubber band. Allow the rubber band to snap back on to all four fingers. Do not let anyone see you insert your fingers into the loop at any time. Try to time it so that, as you turn your hand down, the band snaps and your fingers go in at the same time.

**3** Show your audience the back of your hand. With all your fingers curled down it looks like the rubber band is only around your first and middle fingers.

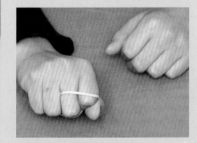

**4** Straighten all your fingers quickly in your left hand. The rubber band seems to jump to your other two fingers!

### ⭐ TOP TIP!
Experiment in front of a mirror to see if it looks believable. Also, try it with sizes of rubber bands with different elasticity to find what works best for you. After practicing, try to do it very fast. It will look like you just flicked your hand and the rubber band jumped.

# BAND ON EAR

## Effect

With this trick, an rubber bands flies into the air and is caught on the performer's ear. To prepare, you need to secretly hook a rubber band over your ear so it is unnoticed as you talk to the audience.

| Wow factor | ★ ★ ☆ ☆ ☆ |
|---|---|
| Performance skills | ★ ★ ★ ★ ☆ |
| Skill | ★ ☆ ☆ ☆ ☆ |
| Time to learn | 15 minutes |
| Set up time | 1 minute |

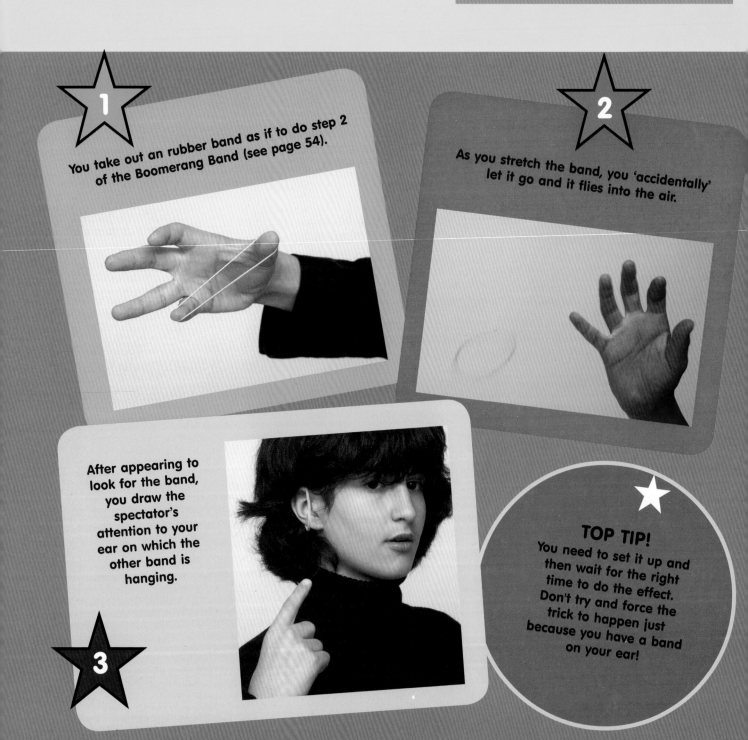

**1** You take out an rubber band as if to do step 2 of the Boomerang Band (see page 54).

**2** As you stretch the band, you 'accidentally' let it go and it flies into the air.

**3** After appearing to look for the band, you draw the spectator's attention to your ear on which the other band is hanging.

### TOP TIP!
You need to set it up and then wait for the right time to do the effect. Don't try and force the trick to happen just because you have a band on your ear!

## Effect

Two rubber bands separate from each other mysteriously. This is a baffling and quite visible illusion. To prepare, you need two rubber bands the same size. They should not be flat-shaped.

| Wow factor | ★ ★ ★ ★ ★ |
|---|---|
| Performance skills | ★ ★ ★ ★ ★ |
| Skill | ★ ★ ★ ★ ★ |
| Time to learn | 1 hour |
| Set up time | None needed |

**1**

Place one rubber band around the left thumb and forefinger. Your fingers should make a C formation. Make the rubber band tight between your fingers. Point these fingers toward your audience.

**2**

Drape the other rubber band over your first finger on the right hand and lower it behind the other rubber band. Slip your right thumb into the bottom of the draped rubber band. The back of your right hand should be facing your audience. This is the locked position. From here it should look as if there is no way the rubber bands can separate.

**3**

Stretch the rubber bands, showing that they are behind each other. Also, move the rubber band to the side, showing they can't escape over the thumb or finger.

**4**

Do this a few times to lull your spectators. Then stretch the rubber bands back towards your wrist. The middle finger of the right hand slips through the bottom part of the rubber band and your thumb releases it.

**5**

This should be hidden by the back of your right hand. The audience has seen you make the same motions twice already so they don't expect anything. Your thumb comes up and places itself next to your right forefinger, Slide your forefinger under the band on your thumb. Bring your hands back together and the rubber band slips off your middle finger as you separate your forefinger and thumb.

**6**

Wave your hands magically and separate the rubber bands.

## Effect

The trick is to shoot a rubber band, have it land on the floor and roll all the way back to you. To prepare, first, get some rubber bands, preferably number 16 size. If you can't get that specific one, look for a skinny, round one. The diameter of the circle should be about 1³/4 in/4.5cm.

| Wow factor | ★ ★ ★ ★ ★ |
| --- | --- |
| Performance skills | ★ ★ ★ ★ ★ |
| Skill | ★ ★ ★ ★ ★ |
| Time to learn | 1.5 hours |
| Set up time | None needed |

**1**

Hold your hand with the fingers spread out, especially the little finger and thumb. They should be spread as far as possible.

**2**

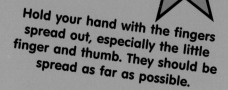

Place the palm of your hand towards you with the index finger pointing upward and the pinkie and thumb out sideways. Put the rubber band over the end of your little finger, underneath the nail, but if you have long nails, don't wedge it under. The other end of the rubber band goes under your thumbnail, but the bottom half of the rubber band should be stretched completely tight. This, of course, makes the top part very loose.

**3**

Now grab the top part of the rubber band near your thumb and pull towards your little finger and down slightly.

**4**

Your index finger needs to push down at the middle of the rubber band. This should make the rubber band tight on the bottom and tight on the top half nearest your thumb. Please note that all the loose rubber should be on the top between your index finger and your little finger.

**5**

Push down on the middle with your index finger and move your thumb forward so that the rubber band forms an acute angle (about 60 degrees). Hold everything still and pull your thumb out to shoot the rubber band. It should shoot out about 10ft/3m, land on the ground and roll back to you.

## Effect

You appear to do the impossible and tie a knot in a rope or even a tie without letting go of the ends. No matter how hard your audience try and catch you out they won't, as long as you practice. This is also known as WG Hunter's Impossible Knot.

| | | |
|---|---|---|
| Wow factor | | ★★★★★ |
| Performance skills | | ★★★★★ |
| Skill | | ★★★★★ |
| Time to learn | 45 minutes | |
| Set up time | None needed | |

**1**

Hold the rope or tie at both ends. Move your right hand behind your left forearm and pull the rope over it.

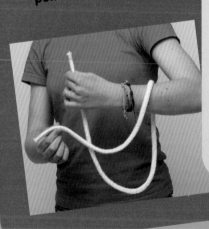

**2**

Take the rope around and back through the large loop.

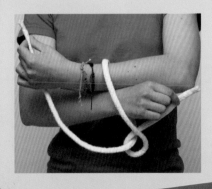

**3**

Bring it back around the center rope and through the loop to the position shown.

Having done this, the rope continues to fall off your wrists and hands, and a knot will be formed in the center. This should be a smooth, simple action that is done without looking at the rope.

**5**

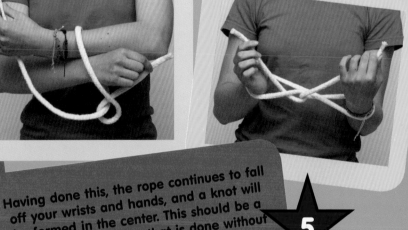

Now you appear to let the rope fall from your wrists as you drop the rope off your hands. However, under the cover of tilting your hands, you actually let go of the right-hand end, and take hold of the rope close to your little finger.

**4**

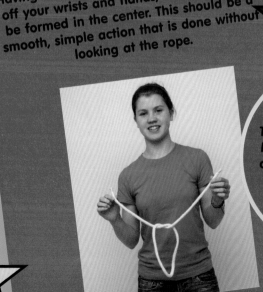

**TOP TIP!**
The big action hides the little action. You should do this without looking at your hands.

## Effect

A 5ft/1.5m rope is displayed and examined by the audience. The magician holds both ends together to locate the center of the rope. The rope is cut in two and the cut ends tied together. Then the knot is removed from the rope which, amazingly, is again in one piece.

| Wow factor | ★★★★★ |
|---|---|
| Performance skills | ★★★★★ |
| Skill | ★★★★★ |
| Time to learn | 1 hour |
| Set up time | None needed |

**1** After the rope is examined hold both ends in your left hand. Reach through the hanging loop with your right index finger just left of the center.

**2** With your thumb and middle finger on the outside of the loop, lift the center as if to place it in your left hand.

**3** As your right hand approaches your left hand, reach through the loop with your right thumb and middle finger and grab a few inches below the end and pull it through the loop.

Bring the loop up into your left hand, hiding the real center of the rope in the palm of your left hand.

**4**

**6**

Tie a knot in the short piece at its location in the middle of the long piece and it will look like two halves of the rope tied together. To restore the rope just slide the knot off one end.

The audience thinks they see both ends and the middle of the rope above your left fist. Cut the loop and hold both ends of the small piece that you cut off, letting the other ends fall.

**5**

Ask an adult to cut the rope.

## Effect

This is a classic magic trick. The performer takes a spool of thread and unravels about an arm's length. The thread is broken into six or seven pieces, then, holding one piece in one hand, the other pieces are rolled into a ball and 'squashed' on to a piece that has been hidden in the other hand. When the thread is unraveled it is seen to be completely restored to its original length.

| | |
|---|---|
| Wow factor | ★★★★★ |
| Performance skills | ★★★★★ |
| Skill | ★★★☆☆ |
| Time to learn | 1.5 hours |
| Set up time | None needed |

## Preparation

You need a spool of cotton thread, preferably brightly colored. It has to be cotton, otherwise you will need scissors to cut it. Before you approach the spectator, you must prepare the thread. Unravel just over an arm's length (note: this will be the same length as the piece you will take off later). DO NOT SNAP THIS OFF THE SPOOL. Make a tiny ball of thread out of this length of thread, leaving about 2in/5cm before the ball.

**1** Take the spool and unravel about an arm's length of thread. You will already have the ball of thread (hidden) plus the 2in/5cm showing, in your right hand, and an arm's length of thread and then the spool in your left hand.

**2** Approach a spectator. Break off the arm's length of thread from the spool, and give them the spool to hold.

Break the first piece of thread off – about 5in/13cm. Now the piece in your right hand looks like a 5in/13cm length. Thanks to the hidden ball, it is it is just over an arm's length – this will be your restored thread.

**3** It now looks as though you are holding half an arm's length, when in fact, thanks to the ball hidden between your index finger and thumb (right hand), you have just over two arm's lengths.

**5** The pieces in your left hand can be broken as many times as you like. Clearly show the thread to be broken.

**6** Now, by rubbing your left hand thumb and index finger together, make a ball of the pieces of thread and 'squash' the 5in/13cm thread from your right hand on to the ball. At the same time, tuck in the left hand ball so it's hidden between your index finger and thumb.

**4**

**7** Now the ball you have been hiding during the whole trick is visible. It looks like the ball you just made out of the broken thread and can be unraveled and is restored. To make the trick believable give it to the spectator as a souvenir.

## 1089 - A FORCE

This is a great way to force a particular number: 1089. Because of the way it uses maths, it will always be 1089.

Ask the spectator to write down a 3-digit number, for example, 853. Now ask them to reverse the number (358). They must then subtract the smaller number from the bigger (853 - 358). Take this new total (495) and again reverse it (594) and add the two together (594 + 495). The result is 1089.

The number is always the same so don't do this to the same spectators more than once. You can reveal a predication of the number however you like.

## BOOK PREDICTION

Find a book with more than 120 pages. Go to page 108 and the first word on line 9. Remember this word.

Explain to the spectator you can read minds. Ask them to select a page and word at random but say you need to tune into their thought waves as they do some maths. Force 1089. Then ask them to go to page 108, look at line 9 and concentrate on the first word. Then reveal the word, letter by letter.

## MAGIC SUGAR CUBE

You need a sugar cube, a pencil and a glass of water. Ask a spectator to pick a number between one and ten and write it on the sugar cube with the pencil. Take the cube between your thumb and finger, making sure your thumb is on the side with the number, and squeezing as hard as possible. The number will transfer to your thumb. Drop the cube into the water. Take the spectator's hand, making sure to place your thumb in their palm. The number will then transfer to their hand. Move their hand over the glass of water. Remove yours and ask them to look at their palm – where they'll see their chosen number!

## IT ADDS UP

Multiply the current year by two. Write this number on a piece of paper and seal it inside an envelope. (For example, if it is 2007, write 4014.) Give a spectator another piece of paper and ask him to write down his year of birth, followed by a year in the past that something – anything - important happened to him. Next, he should write down his age and the number of years it's been since the important event happened. Add these four numbers up, then open the envelope – the total will be exactly the number sealed inside!

## A HAUNTED BOX

You take a matchbox and place it on your hand where it appears to stand unaided. Before you start the trick, take a matchbox and tape a piece of thin fishing wire to the bottom inside of it. Tie a paper clip to the other end of the wire and clip it on your trousers. Place the wire so it goes under your arm and through your fingers.

Play around with it and you can get the matchbox to move, stand up by itself and even open. All you have to do is slowly straighten your arm and watch the box move.

## GET KNOTTY

Try using string, rope or a long shoelace for this challenge. Lay it on the table and ask someone to try and pick up each end and tie a knot in the string without letting go of the ends. Once they have tried, fold your arms and then pick up each end in one of your hands – as you unfold your arms a knot appears in the rope.

## APPEARING KNOT

This is a good stunt. You appear to flick a rope or string and put a knot in it. Before you start, put a knot in a piece of string – that's about 3ft/1m long – about 4in/10cm from the end. Hold this knot in your hand and flick the rope a couple of times. To do the trick, as you flick the rope up catch the other end and release the knot.

## ALL TIED UP

Select two helpers then tie the ends of a rope, tie or string around each wrist of the first helper. This is repeated with the second helper but, before tying the last wrist, the ropes are linked together. The helpers are challenged to separate without removing the ropes, cutting them or undoing the knots. After lots of fun and confusion, show them how easy it is.

To separate them, take the middle of one rope up through the loop around the other person's wrist. This rope should be on the palm side of the wrist. Pull enough rope through the loop to go over the hand and then pull it out on the back side of the hand. The two helpers will now be free of each other.

## LINKING PAPER CLIPS

For this you need a piece of paper or a banknote, and two paper clips. Fold the note in half along the short edges. Then make a zig zag shape. Place one paper clip on one edge and the middle piece and the other on the opposite edge and middle piece. If you pull the ends of the note sharply, the paper clips leap off and appear to have joined themselves together!

## JUMPING STICKS

For this you need two cocktail sticks. Hold one in your right hand. Pinch it between the thumb and first finger about two-thirds along the match from the head. The fingernail of the middle finger is under the end of the cocktail stick. A second cocktail stick is in your left hand. Rub your right-hand match on your arm or clothes. Now bring the sticks together and, as they touch, the left-hand stick jumps into the air. The secret is that, as the sticks touch, your right-hand middle finger is clicked causing the other stick to jump. Practice the timing for this.

## MR FREEZE

It appears that you pour water into a cup and it turns into ice. Have a plastic cup with a piece of kitchen or toilet roll in the bottom, and on top of this place an ice cube. Don't show people the inside of the cup. Pour a little water in the cup, blow on it using your magic breath and then tip out the ice cube. The paper should absorb the water – but remember not to use too much.

## NUTTY EARRING

You need a couple of peanuts in their shells for this. Take a peanut, still in the shell, and squeeze the top. The join in the shell should crack open. Keeping the gap open, pinch it on to their earlobe and release.

## MAGIC MESSAGE

Try putting a little bit of pencil lead under your thumb nail. Now hold a pad in your hand by you side, practice writing simple words and numbers. When you can do this, you are ready to perform. Take a pencil and pretend to write a name of a piece of fruit on the pad, say it is a prediction and ask the spectator to name any fruit. As they do, secretly using the nail write the name of the fruit – and show them the prediction!

## RISING RING

This requires a similar set-up to the Haunted Box page 58. Get a pencil or pen and, using a small spot of glue, secure a piece of thin fishing wire on the end of the pen. Tie a paper clip to the other end of the wire and clip it on your pants or a jacket button. Place the wire so it goes under your arm and through your fingers.

Borrow a ring from a spectator and, holding the pen in your right hand, place the ring over the pen. Focus on the ring and slowly straighten your arm – the ring rises up the pen. Amazing! Note: with these rising tricks you might have better results with a strong, thin black cotton, but be careful it doesn't show up against your clothes.

## WEIRD PENDULUM

You need a pendulum – either a string with a weight, or a chain and ring both work well. You can hold the pendulum yourself, but it is best to get someone else to hold it. Ask the person holding the pendulum a question. Tell them that, if the answer is yes, it will swing in a straight line, if it's no it will swing in a circle. Without any help the pendulum will move. Even if you asked the person to hold the pendulum still they couldn't – no matter how hard they try to keep it steady, it will continue to answer every question!

# CHAPTER 6

The ability to fly, float or be weightless fascinates us and is something magicians have been doing in different ways for centuries.

Famous examples include the Floating Light Bulb of Harry Blackstone Jnr and Losander's floating table. The floating of an assistant or the levitation of the magician, be it David Blaine in the street or David Copperfield flying around the theater, has the ability to astound and amaze.

This chapter scratches the surface, with three illusions for you to try. They are often more about controlling where the audience is, managing it, talking to it and setting up the 'miracle', as much as the actual method.

Many levitation effects, in common with most magic, also need the performer to act well. You need to believe what you are doing is real – if you don't, you will never convince your audience.

## Effect

The performer stands at an angle facing away from the audience and appears to levitate a few inches above the ground. The effect generally does not last for more than five seconds. The performer's feet return to the ground, and the effect is complete.

| | |
|---|---|
| Wow factor | ★ ★ ★ ★ ★ |
| Performance skills | ★ ★ ★ ★ ★ |
| Skill | ★ ★ ★ ★ ★ |
| Time to learn | 1 hour |
| Set up time | None needed |

**1**

Start by telling your audience that you are going to try and do the impossible and make yourself lighter than air. You need to prepare a space, as it requires thought and concentration from you.

**2**

Stand in front of the audience, with your back facing away. They should be 3-6ft/1-2m away, with your body positioned at about a 45-degree angle to them.

**3**

Use your hidden right toes to slowly push yourself up a few inches, keeping your heels together. Try to be subtle when doing this. Don't just say, "I'm going to float now." Instead say, "Now watch my feet closely", to make the person focus on the illusion. Make sure everyone is viewing you from one side.

**4**

Remember to keep the heel of the foot which is closest to the audience level with the ground, to provide a sense of acutal levitation.

**5**

Hold the position for two or three seconds, then let yourself down quickly, avoiding sudden moves or shudders. Look like it has taken a lot of mental effort. When you land, bend your knees and take a step forward.

# CUP LEVITATION

## Effect

The magician announces that he or she is going to make an empty cup float. Releasing their grip on the cup and it appears to float in mid-air.

| Wow factor | ★★★★★ |
|---|---|
| Performance skills | ★★★★★ |
| Skill | ★★★★★ |
| Time to learn | 1 hour |
| Set up time | None needed |

**1** Before confronting your audience, take a large empty paper or styrofoam cup. Carefully make a hole in one side of the empty cup, big enough for your thumb to stick through.

**2** Hold the empty cup with both your hands and, facing the others in your party, announce that you are going to try and make the cup float.

**3** Have one thumb pushed through the nearest side of the cup to you, out of view of your audience. Then, appear to be concentrating your mind on the cup and gradually open up both hands at the same time.

**4** While doing this, push your hands slightly forward as if you are following the floating cup.

**5** Eventually grab the cup with both hands. Now, discreetly slip your thumb out from the side of the cup.

### TOP TIP!
This is a simple illusion but it looks great when done at the right angle. Practice in front of a mirror to make sure that you get the angle and timing right. After all, if you don't believe the cup is floating, why would your audience?

### Extra Trick!
Using the same principle as the floating cup, try putting a small bit of double-sided tape on the center of a banknote. When you appear to hold it against your right hand with your left, bend the middle finger of your right hand and touch it on to the tape. Slowly remove your left hand and the note appears to float.

## FLOATING STRAW

Static electricity can be very useful. This trick requires a plastic straw in a wrapper. Try different kinds of straw to see which works best for you.

First tear off the tip of the wrapper and throw it away. Now you have to get a static charge on the straw. Grip the straw at the tip with the fingers of one hand and, firmly squeezing the wrapper with the fingers of the other hand, pull the straw from the wrapper as quickly as possible and drop the wrapper on the table. Now slowly wave the straw over the end of the wrapper. The straw wrapper should sway around by itself as if hypnotized. And sometimes you can even get it to hang off the end of the straw.

If the static starts to wear off, recharge the wrapper by stroking it briskly along the straw.

## HAIR RAISING

If you have a friend with long hair, try rubbing a balloon against your shirt and holding it near to their hair – the static electricity will make it stand on end!

## FLOATING MONEY

Thread can be very useful for floating objects. Use black linen thread – about 40in/1m long. Attach one end to the top of your shirt or jacket and let the other hang loose with a bit of putty on it. As you sit down at a table or stand next to a wall, attach the putty to a table or solid object and practice getting the thread into your hands between the thumb and first finger. Borrow a banknote – a $1 or £5 – and screw it up into a ball. As you do so, make sure the thread goes through the ball. Now move your hands and the ball appears to float. You must do this with dark thread against a dark background.

## RISING BREAD

Take a bread roll and push a fork into its side. Now, hold the end of the fork in your right hand between your middle and ring finger and practice moving it about. Lay it on the table and cover it with a napkin or light cloth. Now pick up the cloth corners in your right and left hand. As you pick up the right corner, also pick up the fork and slowly make the bread rise up and dance about. As you get better at this you can put the bread on the fork as you cover it with a napkin.

## TRICK LIST